To A Fabulous Son and equally amazing
Daughter - Lo[...] [...]d
at an approp[...]

Love You Marie
xxx

To Matilda and Grace:
I think you're both almost at an age now when you can scrape
the dog poo off your own shoes and bike wheels don't you?

Dog Poo on the Wheels Trike

Another laugh-out-cry-out-loud book for Mums

NEW HOLLAND

Words by Penny Attiwill

Illustrations by Sean Roche

First published in New Zealand in 2008 by New Holland Publishers (NZ) Ltd
218 Lake Road, Northcote, Auckland 0627, New Zealand
www.newhollandpublishers.co.nz

ISBN: 978 1 86966 214 1

Publishing manager: Matt Turner
Design: Richard Seakins, Parkhouse / Justine Mackenzie

A catalogue record for this book is available from the National Library of New Zealand.

Copyright © Goose Books Pty Ltd 2007
PO Box 190 (Level 1, 195 Lennox Street)
Richmond Victoria 3121 Australia

10 9 8 7 6 5 4 3 2 1

Printed by SNP Leefung in China, on paper sourced from sustainable forests.

To all the mums who find motherhood a bit of an emotional, physical and mental roller-coaster ride, this book is for you.

You are not alone.

Oops you did it again!

It's now obvious that every time you have sex
you conceive a baby.

And every time you have a baby
your brain shrinks just that little bit more.

It is now the size of a dried fig.

This doesn't stop your three-year-old asking
worldly, unanswerable questions
whenever you're a sitting duck for his attention.

Thank goodness for child care.

After 495 days on a waiting list
you can now look forward to Mondays and Wednesdays
just enjoying those oh-so-very-special,
lazy, hazy days with a newborn ...

... of course this is only possible
when things are running absolutely smoothly.

You're not the first mum to try this on
and the youthful, childless child care worker
won't have a bar of it.

After being threatened with having you and your child removed from the centre you slink your way down to pick him up and face a frosty reception.

You spend the next 48 hours knee deep in vomit and diarrhoea. You place your projectile-pooing baby in a safe place while you go searching for clean pyjamas for your eldest child.

This takes some time because you mistakenly walk into the bathroom instead and then can't remember what you're looking for.

Things need to change on the homefront
now that you are a family of four.
You can't go on like this.

You swing into action and write a list
that goes on the wall with all the other lists.

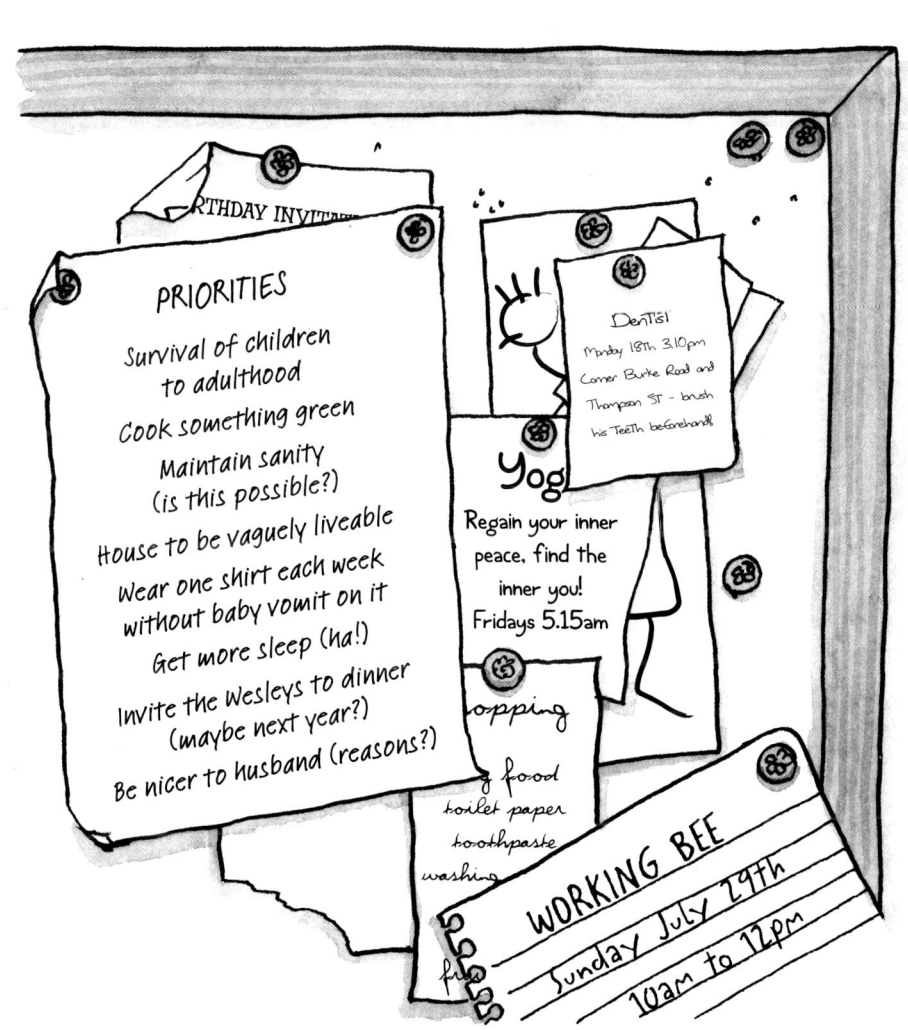

First up you decide to spend every Monday
cooking and freezing large batches of nutritious meals
so that dinners are no longer a boring, tedious, mundane,
dull, monotonous, repetitious, mind-numbing, tiresome,
uninteresting, humdrum, banal, routine challenge.

You also decide to get a cleaner through the house
once a fortnight on a Tuesday
to lighten the load.

"She used my smoochie as a rag and now it doesn't smell like smoochie any more."
"But where on earth did you find her honey? Most cleaners would know not to scour a monitor, surely."
"I have no idea darling. Look under the bed, in the cupboard, on the back patio or in the fridge. I'm sure it's somewhere. Mummy's just busy tidying up after the cleaner."

Wednesdays are going to be wash days.
Perhaps this is a little ambitious since every day
would appear to be wash day, but it's worth giving it a try.

Grocery shopping will happen on a Thursday
even if it means having two children in tow.

This is your biggest challenge each week
and it's not just the children that test you …

... comments from strangers at checkout
can strip you of your last skerrick of self confidence
in close to a nano second.

And Friday? Well Friday is going to be your 'time-out' day.

Your partner jumps at the idea because, as everyone knows,
a happy mummy means a happy daddy.

He suggests an early morning yoga class in the park
should do the trick … then you can be back home by 6.30am
to feed the baby, cook toast fingers and help get him off to work.

You feel a little cheated.
Yoga at dawn just didn't do it for you,
so you book a long-overdue haircut and colour to perk you up.

You give up on the idea of a pamper
until the children start school.

Life would be so much less stressful if Fridays
were spent doing whatever your three-year-old desires.
If this means parks, playgrounds, slides, swings,
more parks, more playgrounds, more slides, more swings
and doing wheelies on his tricycle then so be it.

You'll be able to sit back for an hour or two,
truly relax, unwind and smell the fresh air.

The next day your best friend
(the one who can't discipline her five children all aged under six)
pops over with some handy advice.

As soon as she gathers up her horde and leaves
you do something about it.

Your thoughts start flowing freely.
It all becomes crystal clear.
Being a mum is not easy at times
but you love your kids and that's all that matters.

If anything happened to them you'd be lost, a shadow of a woman.
Just imagine: away on a relaxing family holiday and the balcony
collapses and down they drop 28 floors,
or what if a swarm of bees were to chase them through the park
one day and sting them hundreds of times
and you couldn't catch up to shoo them away,
or what if, on an innocent visit to the zoo,
the fence gave way and the lions mauled them both to death
because they were holding ice-creams, or what if …

Being a mother of two young children
is extremely challenging with a hangover.

But once the hangover lifts you experience a more sober epiphany.

There's no right or wrong way to be a good mum.
You just need to find your own rhythm,
and perhaps the best advice may be not to listen to others' advice …

... and muddle your way through motherhood as best you can.

If this means mucking up on the educational side of things
from time to time then so be it.

Always remembering that what your children don't know won't hurt them.

In fact nine times out of ten you are just trying to protect them from the harsh realities of life in general …

… and from the relentless commercialism in daily life.

The little white lies you tell them here and there are perfectly harmless and surely won't have any long-lasting effects ...

… so long as you mean well and have their best interests at heart.

Occasionally though you stuff up big time
and it all ends in tears.

These events should be put behind you as quickly as possible
and forgotten by all involved parties.

Life is good apart from these small hiccups
and you know you wouldn't give motherhood up for the world.

Guilt trip number 27,945:
Okay, if you were being completely honest here,
you know that if you were offered a three-week stay on an exotic
island with a blue lagoon, a deep-relaxation massage table,
a guaranteed eight-hour sleep through each and every night
and a couple of tanned, muscular waiters offering tantalising cocktails
you would jump at the chance.

But since this little fantasy is never going to eventuate
you really need to let it go.

There are always going to be special moments
to look forward to with your children.

You know those moments when you cry as you say you love them,
when you cry as you say you'll be their mummy forever,
when you cry because Charlotte's Web is such a sad, sad film,
when you cry because you just can't stop crying.

These are the times when your child brings out the very best in you.

You're oozing with love.
You're a fulfilled woman.
You're generous, caring, nurturing and playful.

In fact there are even some days when you're sure
you impress your children with your youthfulness.

But then there are other days
when you really don't feel on top of things …

… days when your patience levels reach breaking point.

On a very bad day your bewildered partner
can cop the majority of your wrath.

He now often spends Saturday afternoons trawling the newspaper
looking for a DIY shed kit so that he is assured
of a safe refuge in the garden at all times.

A lovingly cooked evening meal eaten together as a family
always restores domestic peace and harmony.

You pour your heart and soul into cooking bangers, mash and peas
and your family is relieved that you're back to your old self.
The children pop off to bed without a major battle
and your partner decides to test his luck.

You know exactly where it might lead
and because there's absolutely no point tempting fate
and because you wouldn't mind your body being left alone
for 15 consecutive minutes you choose your night attire very carefully.

And so life continues on, day in day out,
in this half-crazed rhythm called family life.

Luckily love, even if not always obvious,
manages to haul everyone through a bad, bad day.

If this book made you laugh - or cry - check out the other titles in the series by Penny Attiwill:

Dog Poo on the Pram Wheels
A laugh-out-cry-out-loud book for mums.
Dog Poo on the Pram Wheels, the prequel to *Dog Poo on the Trike Wheels,* takes a humorous look at those days in a new mum's life that can only be referred to as challenging, frustrating, tiring and at times just plain old bad.

Mummy Doesn't Do It Like That
A laugh-out-cry-out-loud book for dads.
Mummy Doesn't Do It Like That takes a humorous look at those days in a new dad's life that can only be referred to as completely bewildering, overwhelmingly exhausting and at times just outright challenging.

Grandpa Gave Us Chocolate at Bedtime
A laugh-out-cry-out-loud book for grandparents.
Grandpa Gave Us Chocolate at Bedtime takes a humorous look at some of the many challenges grandparents may face when they succumb to a week-long visit by their grandchildren.

NH
NEW
HOLLAND